On It, Phonics! Consonant Blends

Bring the Bread
The BR Blend

By Connor Stratton

level 1
little blue readers

www.littlebluehousebooks.com

Little Blue House is distributed by North Star Editions:
sales@northstareditions.com | 888-417-0195

Produced for Little Blue House by Red Line Editorial.

Reading Consultant: Andrew P. Johnson, PhD, Distinguished Faculty Scholar and Professor of Literacy Instruction, Minnesota State University, Mankato

Photographs ©: Shutterstock Images, cover, 5 (branch), 6, 17; iStockphoto, 5 (bread), 5 (brings), 5 (broom), 5 (brown), 9, 11, 13, 15, 19, 21, 23

Library of Congress Control Number: 2023910324

ISBN
978-1-64619-931-0 (hardcover)
978-1-64619-949-5 (paperback)
978-1-64619-983-9 (ebook pdf)
978-1-64619-967-9 (hosted ebook)

Printed in the United States of America
Mankato, MN
102023

About the Author

Connor Stratton writes and edits nonfiction children's books. He lives in Minnesota.

Table of Contents

Consultant Note

"On It, Phonics!" is designed to reinforce vowel sounds, beginning blends, and sight words and to provide reading practice for young readers. Books like these are one important part of a comprehensive literacy program for students at emergent and beginning levels. "On It, Phonics!" should be used with other high-quality children's books. Instructors and parents are advised to go over the words in the picture glossary before students begin reading, and review the sight words after students finish reading. You can also ask students to go back and identify words with the target letter-sound.

Andrew P. Johnson, PhD,
Distinguished Faculty Scholar and
Professor of Literacy Instruction,
Minnesota State University, Mankato

BR Blend Picture Glossary

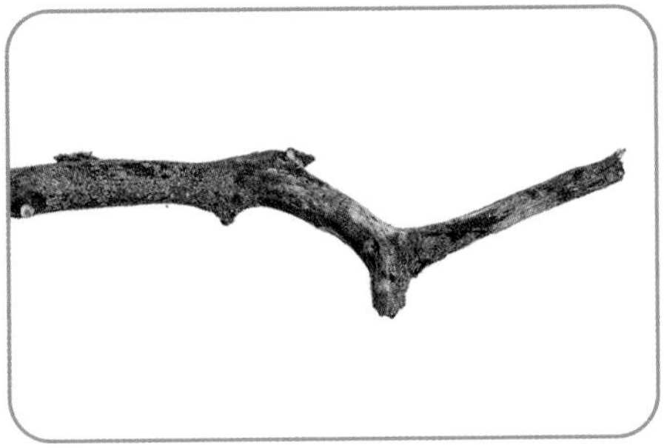

branch

bread

brings

broom

brown

branch

Branch

This is a branch.

This is bread.

bread

This is a broom.

broom

This branch is brown.

brown

This bread is brown.

brown

This broom is brown.

brown

The dog brings a branch.

branch
dog

She brings bread.

bread

He brings a broom.

broom

Sight Words

a
brown
he
is
she
the
this